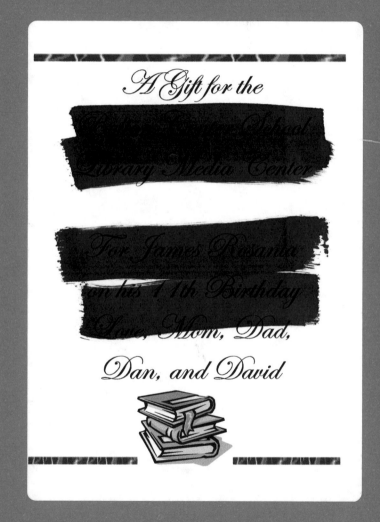

A Gift for the

████████████████

~~████ ████ School~~

~~Library Media Center~~

████████████████

~~For James Rosania~~

████████████████

~~on his 11th Birthday~~

████████████████

~~Love, Mom, Dad,~~

Dan, and David

GUTS

OUR DIGESTIVE SYSTEM

SEYMOUR SIMON

HarperCollins*Publishers*

Special thanks to Shannon Orr, a doctoral student
at Lake Erie College of Osteopathic Medicine,
for reviewing the content of this book.

PHOTO CREDITS

Permission to use the following photographs is gratefully acknowledged: page 4, © by Vero/Carlo/Photo Researchers, Inc.; pages 7 (background), 16, 31, and 32, © by Howard Sochurek, Inc.; page 7 (inset), © by Dr. Dennis Kunkel/Visuals Unlimited; page 8, © by Gladden Willis, M.D./Visuals Unlimited; pages 11 and 23 (background), © by L. Bassett/Visuals Unlimited; page 12 (background), © by Zephyr/Photo Researchers, Inc.; pages 12 (inset) and 23 (inset), © by SIU/Visuals Unlimited; page 15, © by CNRI/Photo Researchers, Inc.; page 19, © by A. Pasieka/Photo Researchers, Inc.; page 20, © by Susumu/Nishinaga, Photo Researchers, Inc.; page 24, © by Carolina Biological/Visuals Unlimited; page 27, © by Susan Leavines/Photo Researchers, Inc.; page 28 (background), © by SPL/Photo Researchers, Inc.; page 28 (inset), © by David M. Martin, M.D./Photo Researchers, Inc.

Library of Congress Cataloging-in-Publication Data
Simon, Seymour.
  Guts : our digestive system / Seymour Simon.— 1st ed.
    p.   cm.
  ISBN 0-06-054651-4 — ISBN 0-06-054652-2 (lib. bdg.)
  1. Gastrointestinal system—Juvenile literature. 2. Digestion—Juvenile
literature. I. Title.
QP145.S499 2005
612.3—dc22   2004014508

7 8 9 10   ❖   First Edition

To my grandkids, Jeremy, Chloe, Benjamin, and Joel
with love from Grandpa Seymour

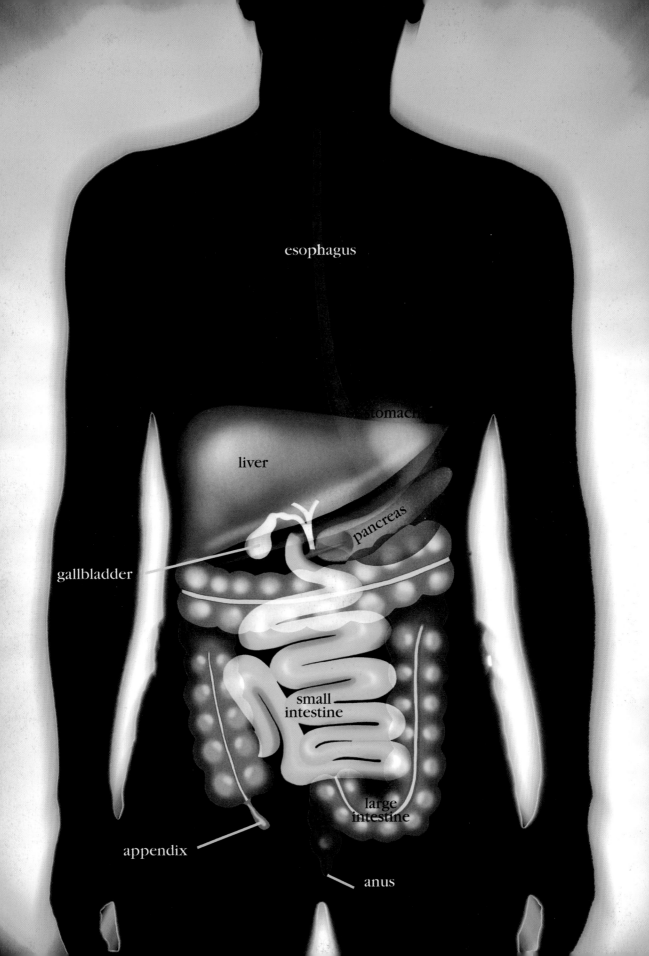

You probably eat three meals and several snacks a day. That adds up to several hundred pounds of food in a year. The digestive system turns the truckload of sandwiches, milk, salads, and pizza that you eat each year into the energy and nutrients that your body needs.

Digestion takes place in a long tube inside the body called the digestive tract, or gut. The digestive tract begins in the mouth and runs through the esophagus, the stomach, and the small and large intestines. Finally the body gets rid of undigested food waste through the anus. Food takes from about twenty to about forty hours to travel through your body.

Your teeth are the hardest parts of your body. They have to be. You use your teeth to bite, tear, chop, and grind the food you eat into smaller pieces that are easier to swallow and digest.

The chisel-shaped front teeth are called incisors. They're used to slice off chunks of food. The pointed canine teeth just beside the incisors are good for ripping and tearing at food. The flat-topped teeth behind the canines are the pre-molars and the molars. Molars are used for chewing and grinding food down into a pulp.

Baby teeth, also called milk or deciduous teeth, begin to break through the gums at the age of about six months. By the time most children are three years old, they have a complete set of around twenty baby teeth. Baby teeth begin to fall out at about six years. By the age of twenty, most people have thirty-two adult teeth, though some people never grow their back molars, called wisdom teeth.

Teeth are covered by hard, white enamel. Enamel can stand years of wear as you bite and grind down hard foods. But if bits of old food and bacteria build up in the mouth, they form a layer of dental plaque. The bacteria in plaque release acids that may cause cavities.

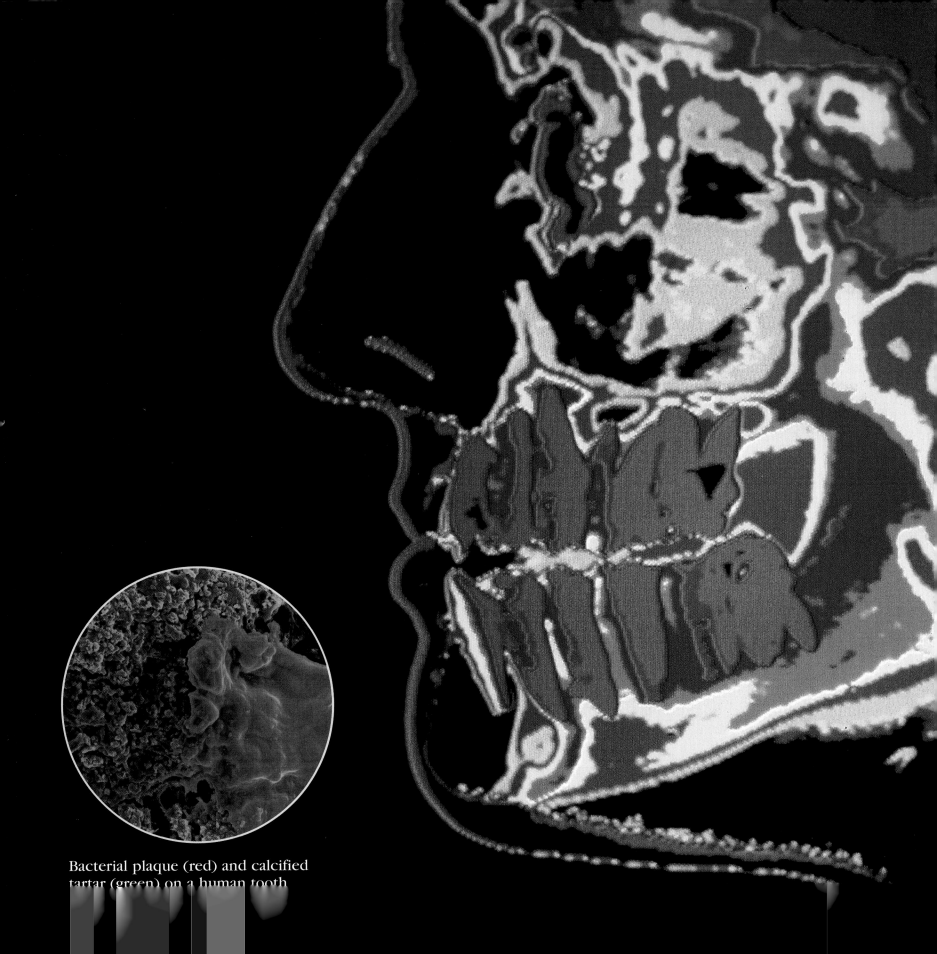

Bacterial plaque (red) and calcified
tartar (green) on a human tooth

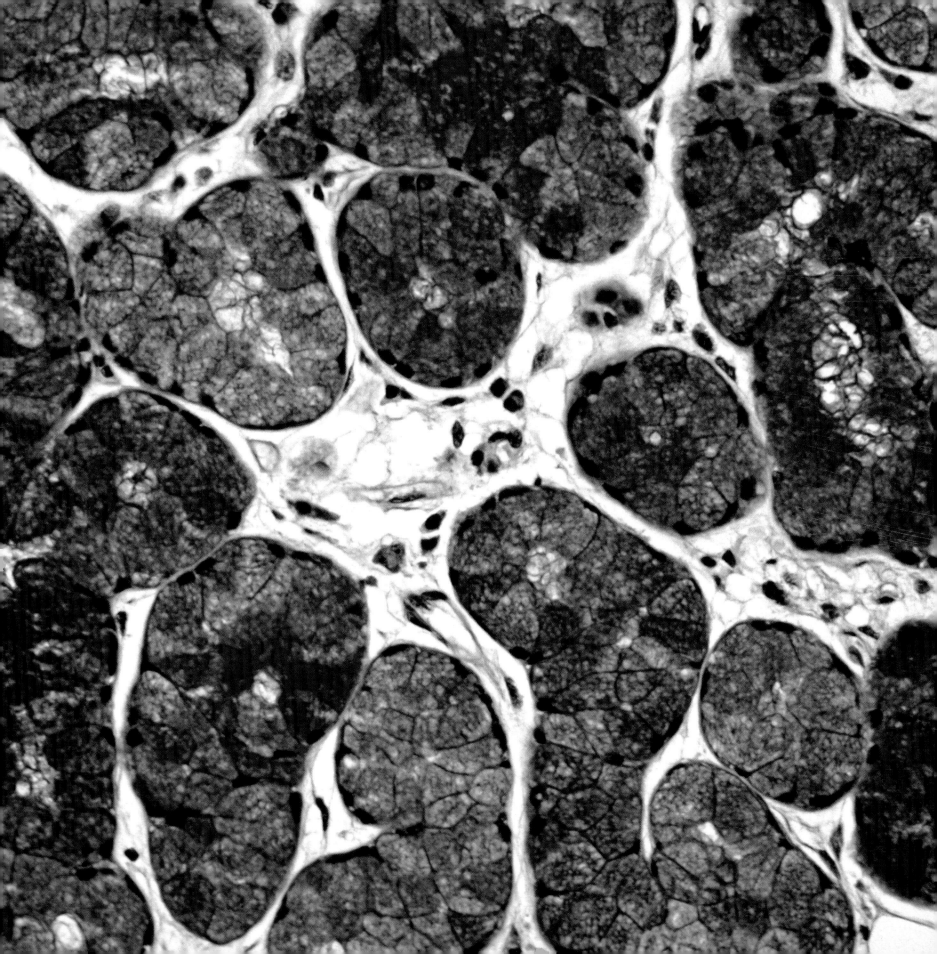

Some animals such as dogs and cats just bolt down food in large chunks. But people need to chew their food slowly so that it can be swallowed and digested. First, taste buds in your tongue check the food in your mouth to make sure you want to eat it. Then your lips and cheeks and tongue push the food back toward the molars.

Chewing crushes and mashes food and mixes it with watery saliva, or spit. As soon as you smell the odor of a food you like, your mouth begins to water, or salivate. Saliva comes from three pairs of salivary glands—at the back of the mouth, under the tongue, and under the sides of the lower jaw. Saliva contains a substance called an enzyme that helps to break down food into nutrients that the body can use. The enzyme in saliva changes starch into sugar.

You can see this for yourself by chewing on a piece of bread and letting it stay in your mouth. Bread is a starchy food without much of a taste. But after a few minutes, the chewed bread will begin to taste sweet. Now try chewing on a piece of non-starchy food such as a peanut or a piece of cheese. These won't taste sweet no matter how long you keep them in your mouth.

A salivary gland made up of mucus glands (with the mucin shown in pink)

The wet lump of chewed food in your mouth is called a bolus. Your tongue presses the bolus backward toward your throat, and you swallow. As soon as you swallow, everything else takes place automatically.

A tube called the esophagus leads down from the back of your throat to your stomach. The top of the esophagus also opens up into your nose. But you certainly don't want food to go up your nose. When you swallow, a flap called the soft palate blocks off the opening to your nose. Lower down, the esophagus opens into a tube that takes air into your lungs. A trapdoor called the epiglottis closes off this opening and prevents food from getting down into your lungs.

When you swallow food, it doesn't just fall down into your stomach. In fact, you can eat standing on your head (don't try it, though; you might choke) and still get food to your stomach. Food is pushed along by two sets of muscles that line the esophagus. The muscles tighten and relax, pushing food along the tube—something like squeezing a tube of toothpaste. This movement is called peristalsis. Thick, slimy mucus coats the inside of the gut and makes it easier for food to slip along.

The esophagus covered in mucus

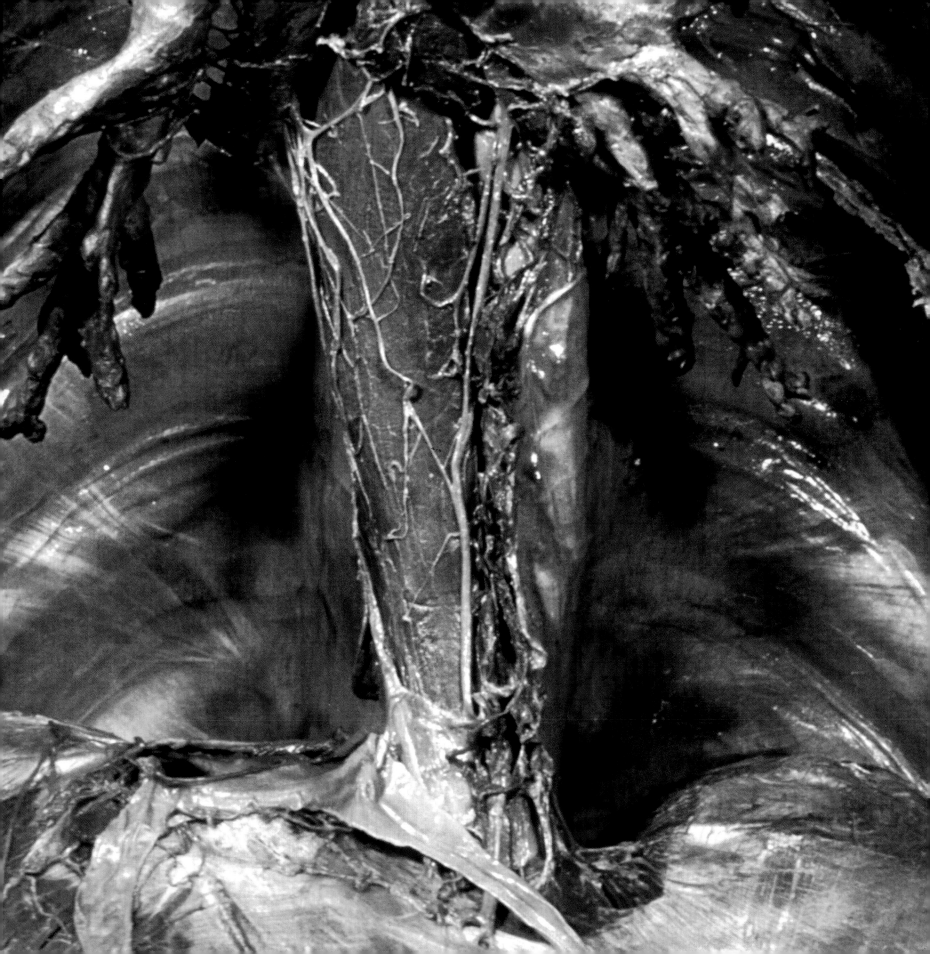

The surface of your stomach looks like this!

Point to your stomach. Surprise! It's not behind your belly button, but higher up, tucked just beneath the left side of your rib cage. An empty stomach is shaped like the letter *J*, and it's only about as big as your fist. Deep, soft folds called rugae line the inside of the stomach. After you eat a meal, the folds flatten out and your stomach swells up. It can get as big as a boxing glove.

Chewed-up food enters the stomach through the esophagus. The food is mixed with a fluid called gastric, or stomach, juice. Three sets of powerful muscles make up most of the stomach wall. The muscles squeeze and tighten about three times a minute, mixing and churning the food inside.

Foods stay in the stomach for different amounts of time. Water passes through very quickly. Meals made up mostly of breads or pasta pass through in an hour or so. But greasy, fatty foods such as double cheeseburgers and fries stay in the stomach for three to four hours or longer. Sometimes if you're sick, you might throw up. In the vomit you can see what food looks like in your stomach. Not very pretty!

Colored X-ray of a healthy stomach

Millions of tiny pits in the walls of the stomach contain glands that produce gastric juice. The stomach produces about eight cups of gastric juice every day. Gastric juice is made up of different substances that help to digest food. One of these, hydrochloric acid, helps to soften food. The acid bath also helps to kill any germs in food. Digestive enzymes and watery mucus make up the rest of gastric juice. Enzymes are body substances that speed digestion.

Hydrochloric acid is so powerful that it could burn a hole in clothing or dissolve an iron nail. So why doesn't it burn holes in the walls of your stomach? The reason is that they are lined with a coating of protective mucus. Even so, the cells wear out quickly and are replaced. Every three or four days, you have an entirely new stomach lining.

In 1822 U.S. Army doctor Dr. William Beaumont treated Alexis St. Martin, who had accidentally shot himself in the stomach. St. Martin recovered from the wound, but the hole remained. For years Beaumont looked into the patient's stomach and experimented with foods to see how they were digested. Beaumont discovered that the stomach produced a strong acid, and many other facts about digestion.

A layer of mucus (yellow) and gastric cells (red) that protects the stomach from digesting itself

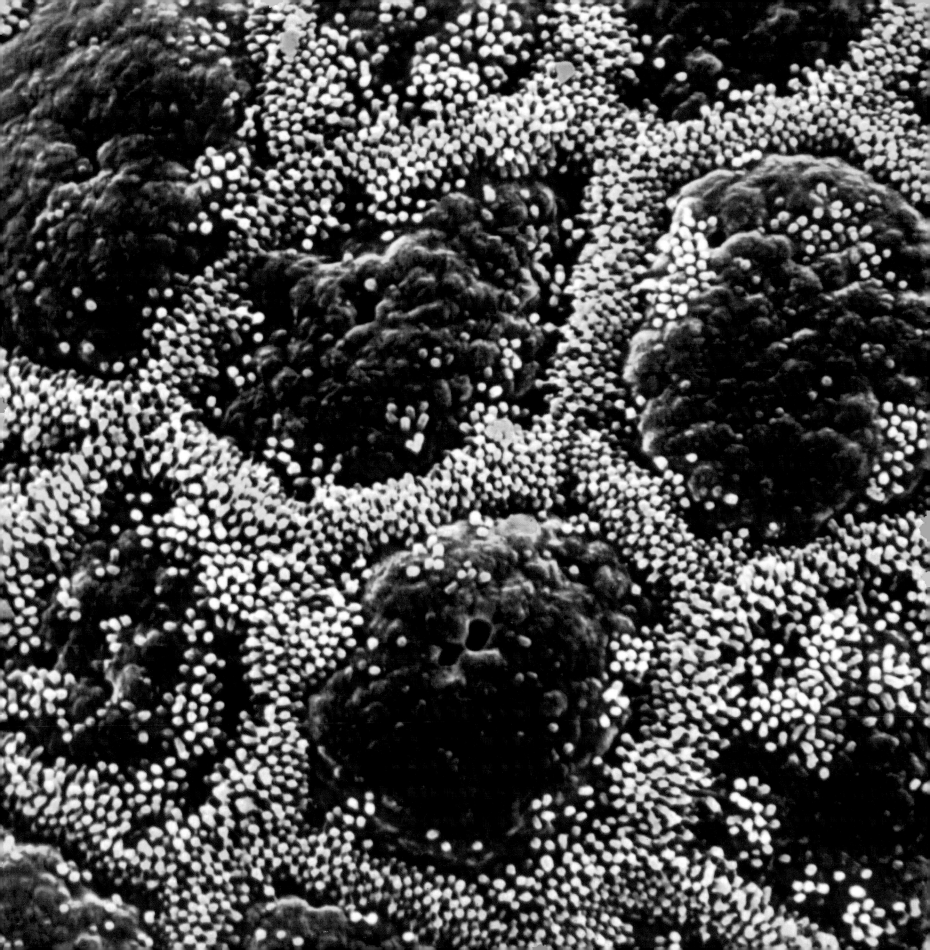

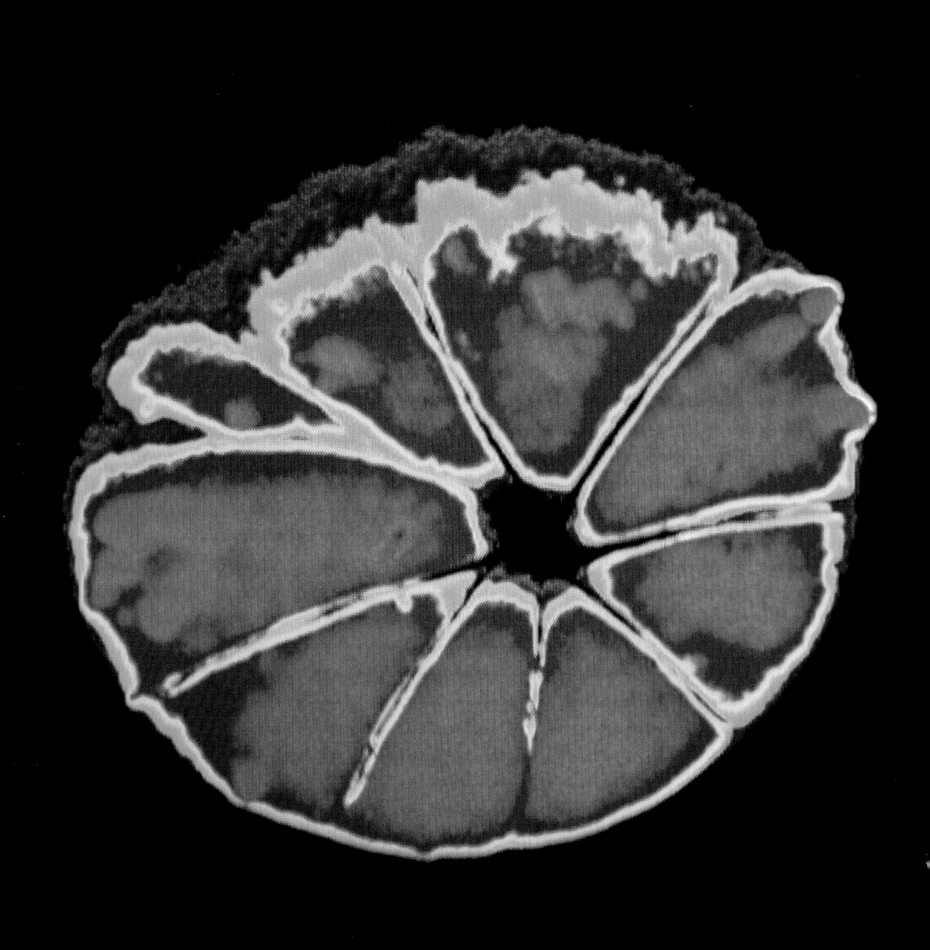

The soupy mixture of food and gastric juices in your stomach is called chyme. Very few food nutrients are absorbed in the stomach. When chyme is liquid enough, peristalsis moves the food downward to the end of the stomach. (Sometimes peristalic waves help to get rid of harmful food that isn't being digested because you are sick or because the food is bad. The waves push food upward through the esophagus and out through your mouth!)

At the bottom of the stomach is a ring of muscles called the pyloric sphincter. When food first enters the stomach, the sphincter is tightly closed so that nothing can leave. As food is digested, the muscles start to relax. With each peristalic wave, a squirt of chyme passes into the small intestine.

This color-enhanced photo of the pyloric sphincter was taken inside the stomach of a living person through a special long, thin, flexible tube called an endoscope. The tube is made of tens of thousands of glass fibers, each about one-fifth the width of a hair. The endoscope is inserted down the mouth and esophagus and inside the stomach so that a doctor can see what's going on inside.

The small intestine is anything but small. In fact, the small intestine is the biggest and most important part of the digestive system. It's called "small" only because it is narrower than the large intestine. The small intestine is about an inch and a half thick and gets to be about twenty feet long. The twenty-foot tube is all folded up and fits inside the mid-section of your body below the rib cage. Food stays in the small intestine for one to six hours. Most digestion happens as food travels through the twists and turns of the small intestine.

The small intestine is made up of three sections that work in different ways. Chyme is squeezed from the stomach into the first section, called the duodenum. The duodenum is shaped like the letter C and is about a foot long. The second section is called the jejunum and is about six and a half feet long. The main work of digestion takes place in the first two sections of the small intestine.

The third and longest section is called the ileum. This is where food nutrients leave the digestive system and are absorbed into the body. By the time food passes out of the small intestine into the large intestine, mostly waste matter is left.

A computer-generated illustration of the stomach and small intestine.

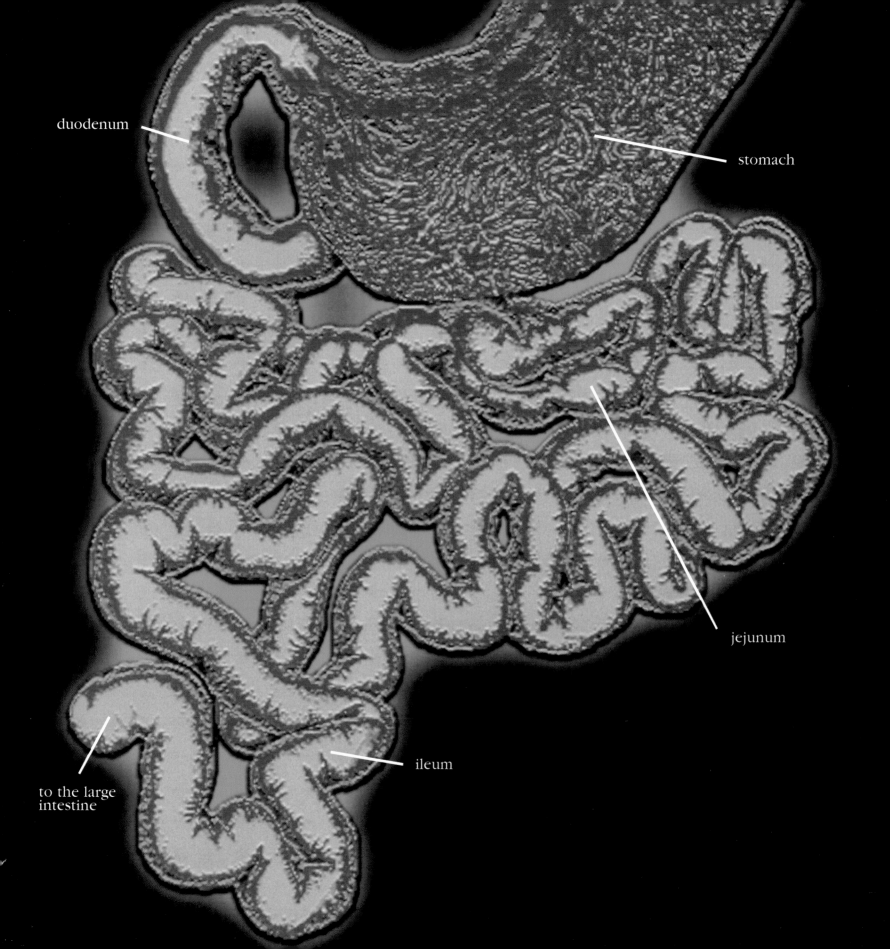

The inner lining of the small intestine is about 2,700 square feet, ten times greater than the area your skin covers and almost the size of a basketball court. That seems like a huge amount of space to fit inside a twenty-foot-long intestinal tube. One of the ways to account for this is that the inside walls are folded and ridged.

But the main explanation is that the inside walls are covered with millions of tiny projections called villi. The villi are covered with even tinier microvilli. All together, the folds, villi, and microvilli make the inside surface of the small intestine about six hundred times greater than it would be if it were smooth.

Villi contain a network of tiny blood vessels called capillaries. Digested proteins and sugars pass through the walls of the villi and through the thin capillary walls into the blood. Villi also contain tiny tubes called lacteals. Digested fat nutrients pass into the lacteals that finally connect with the blood. The villi are always bending and waving like a field of wheat in the wind. The movements help to keep the blood flowing through the capillaries into the bloodstream.

The inner lining of the duodenum, covered in villi

When chyme squirts in from the stomach, cells in the lining of the small intestine start to make intestinal juice. It contains enzymes that help in digesting food nutrients such as proteins, carbohydrates, and fats. Intestinal juice also contains mucus that coats and helps to protect the lining of the small intestine.

The small intestine would be unable to digest food without two other body organs, the pancreas and the liver. The pancreas is about six inches long and looks like a flat pink fish lying behind the stomach. It produces pancreatic juice, a mixture of digestive enzymes, along with a chemical that neutralizes stomach acid.

The liver is the largest internal organ of the body, weighing about three or four pounds. It lies next to the stomach on the right side of your body, just below the rib cage. The liver makes bile, a substance that breaks down globs of fat into tiny droplets that are easier to digest. The bile is stored in a small organ called the gallbladder. The liver and the pancreas each have tubes that join together, sharing a common opening into the duodenum.

Dissected pancreas

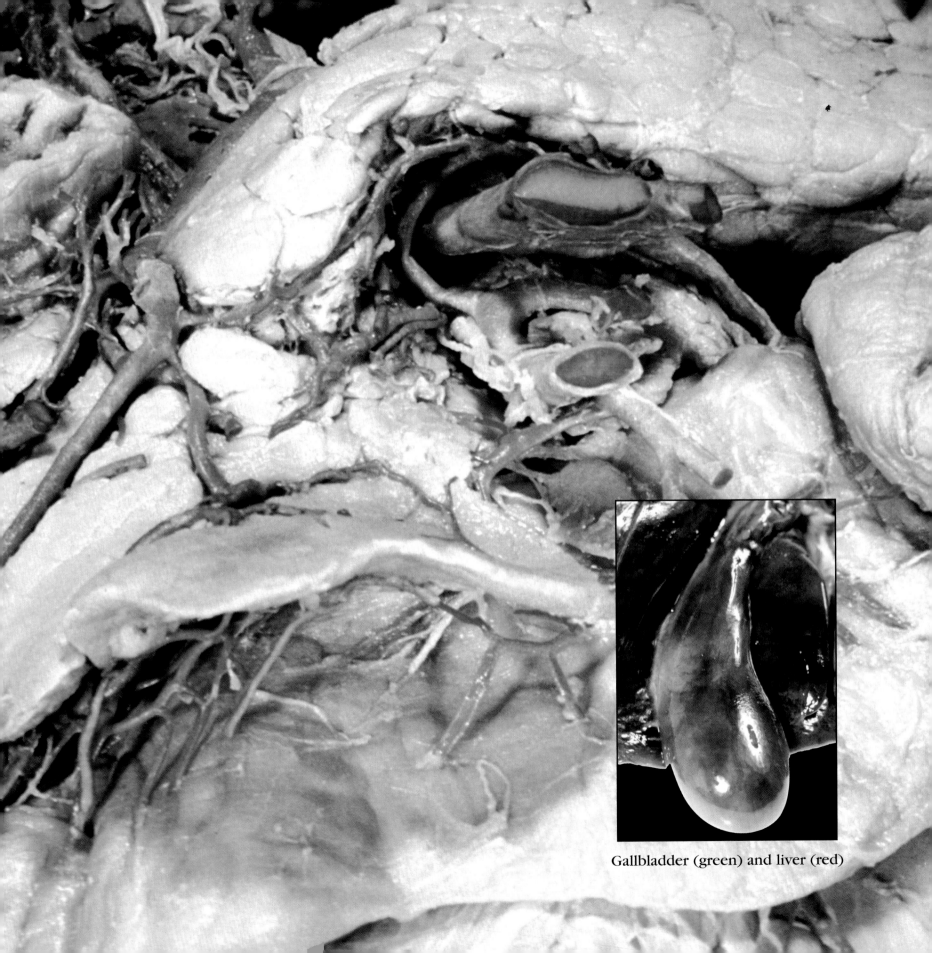

Gallbladder (green) and liver (red)

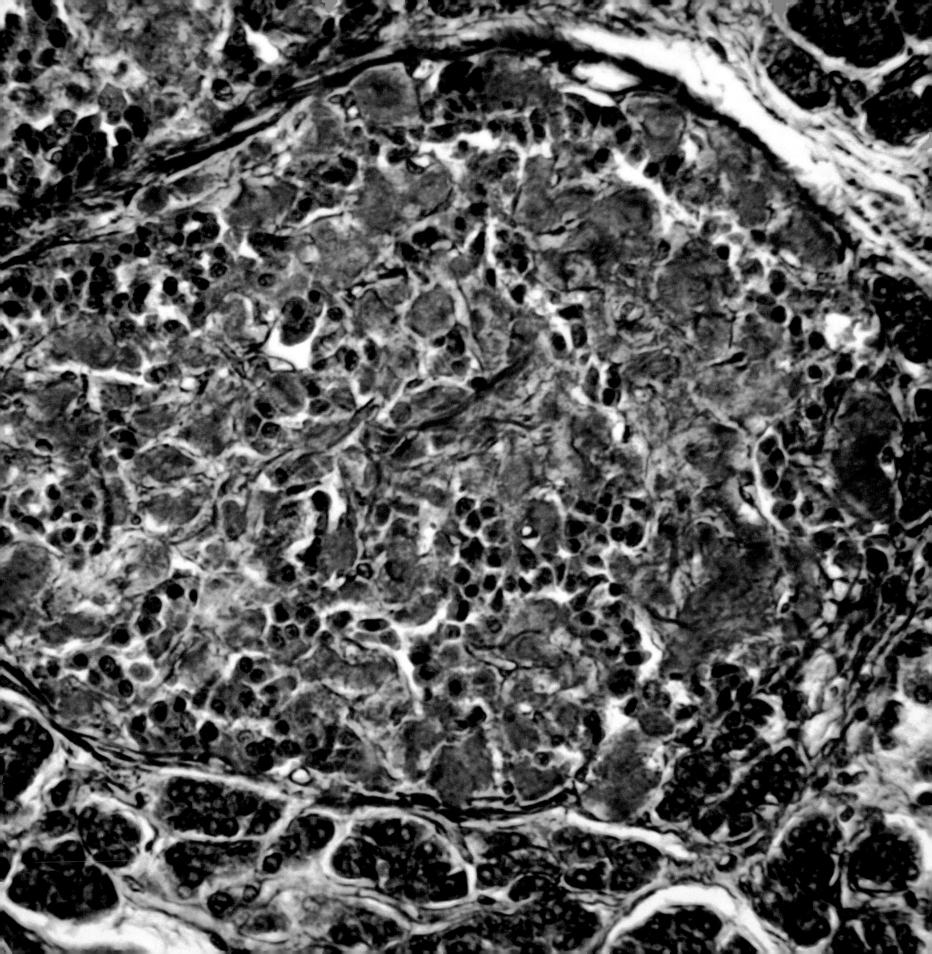

The pancreas and the liver have other important jobs. The pancreas is really two organs in one. It makes pancreatic juice that pours into the small intestine and helps digest foods. The pancreas also makes chemicals called hormones that go into the bloodstream. Hormones help regulate body functions such as energy use and growth.

Insulin is a hormone that is made by the pancreas. Insulin controls how much sugar the body uses for energy immediately and how much is stored for future use. If the pancreas does not produce enough insulin, a person may develop diabetes. Diabetes is a disease in which the sugar level in the blood is not controlled.

The liver is the body's chemical factory. This organ not only produces bile, but it also does hundreds of other jobs in the body. The liver stores sugar in one chemical form and then changes the sugar into another form when the body needs energy. It stores vitamins and iron, filters the blood, and gets rid of poisons and wastes. It also makes parts of the blood and cholesterol. The liver has an amazing ability to repair itself. Even if most of it is injured, the small piece remaining can grow back into a full-size organ.

A microscopic view of the pancreas of someone with diabetes

The large intestine is the last part of the gut. It's much smaller than the small intestine, only about six feet long. But it's called the large intestine because it's two to three inches wide, more than twice as wide as the small intestine.

The first part of the large intestine is the colon. The small intestine joins the colon at the lower right side of your mid-section. The colon goes up the right side, bends sideways below your rib cage, and then turns downward and back to connect with your rectum. The rectum, a straight, five-inch-long tube, leads to the anus, an opening to the outside. A powerful ring of muscles holds the end of the rectum closed.

A lot of water is needed to move food through the gut and help digestion. But the body does not lose the water. As the remains of the food travel through the large intestine, most of the water, along with minerals and vitamins, is absorbed back into the body.

Digested food spends five to ten hours in the large intestine and turns into masses called feces. Feces contain water, undigested food material, dead body cells, and bacteria. Feces are expelled through the anus. This is called defecation, the final part of digestion.

Colored X-ray of the colon, with the loops of the small intestine in the middle

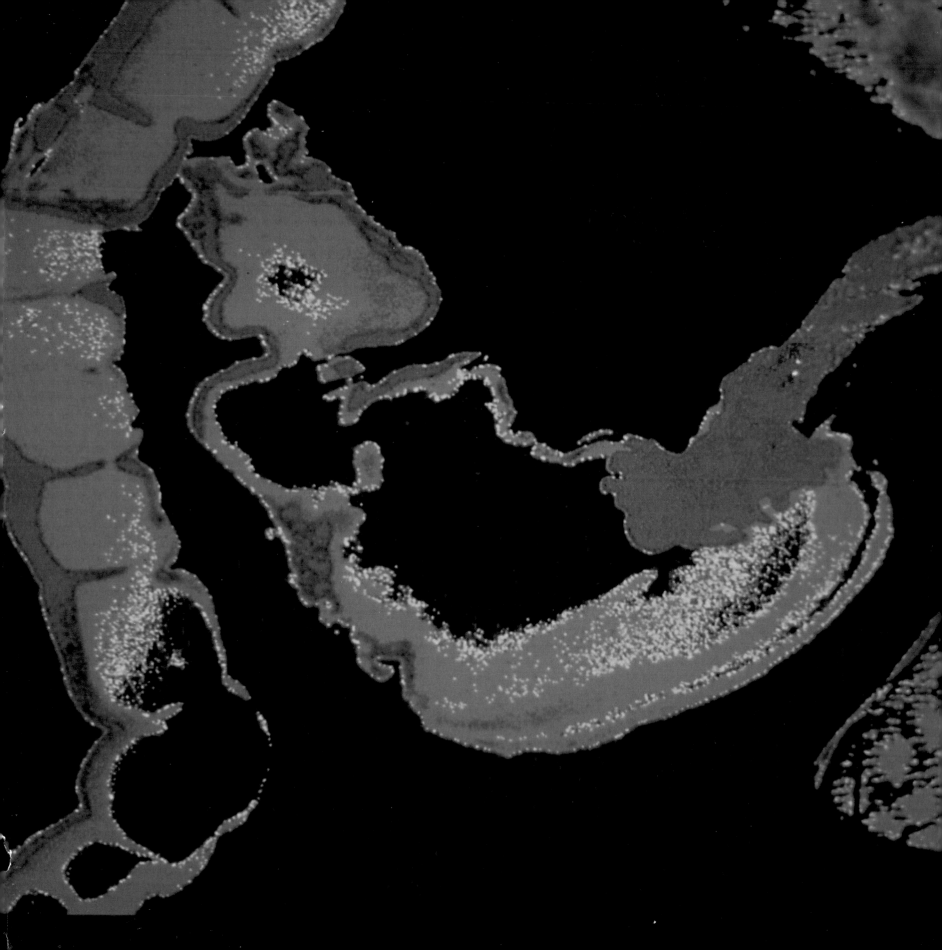

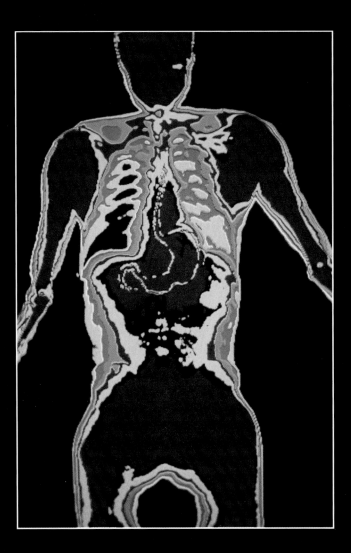

You are what you eat. That doesn't mean that, if you eat a carrot, you will have a carrot growing out of your ear. The food that you eat travels from your mouth to your esophagus, then to your stomach and to your small intestine, and finally to your large intestine and out of your body. Along the way the food is broken down into substances that your body can use. Truly you are made of the fruits and vegetables, cereals and breads, dairy products, meat and fish that are digested in their journey through your gut.